HEAVITREE

of Yesteryear

Chips Barber

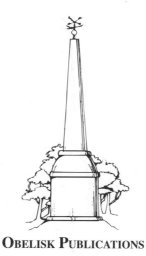

OBELISK PUBLICATIONS

ALSO IN THIS SERIES

Pinhoe of Yesteryear, Parts I & II, *Chips Barber*
The Teign Valley of Yesteryear, Parts I & II, *Chips Barber*
Brixham of Yesteryear, Parts I, II & III, *Chips Barber*
Princetown of Yesteryear, Parts I & II, *Chips Barber*
Kingsteignton of Yesteryear, *Richard Harris*
Ashburton of Yesteryear, *John Germon and Pete Webb*

ALSO BY THE AUTHOR

Around & About the Haldon Hills
The Lost City of Exeter
Diary of a Dartmoor Walker
Diary of a Devonshire Walker
The Great Little Dartmoor Book
The Great Little Exeter Book
Dark & Dastardly Dartmoor
The Ghosts of Exeter
The Great Little Totnes Book
Tales of the Teign
Ten Family Walks on Dartmoor
The Great Little Plymouth Book
Plymouth in Colour
Weird and Wonderful Dartmoor
Ghastly and Ghostly Devon
The South Hams
Torquay
Paignton
Brixham
Ten Family Walks in East Devon

Around & About Salcombe
Around & About Seaton and Beer
Around & About Sidmouth
Around & About Teignmouth and Shaldon
Burgh Island and Bigbury Bay
Beautiful Exeter
Topsham Past and Present
Beautiful Dartmoor
From the Dart to the Start
Dartmouth and Kingswear
Cranmere Pool – The First Dartmoor Letterbox
The Great Little Chagford Book
Haunted Pubs in Devon
The South Hams in Colour
Six Short Pub Walks on Dartmoor
Torbay in Colour – Torquay-Paignton-Brixham
Widecombe – A Visitor's Guide
Newton Ferrers and Noss Mayo
Along the Otter
Films & TV Programmes … Made in Devon

We have over 150 Devon titles – for a list of current books, please contact us at the
address below or telephone Exeter (01392) 468556

PLATE ACKNOWLEDGEMENTS

A great many of the old picture postcard views here are from the collection of Ian Jubb. Thanks
also to Mrs Higgins, Mavis Piller, the Heavitree Brewery, Eddie Drew, Babs Montgomery.

*Dedicated to the memories of Martin Sinclair, Peter Spivey and my old friend
Tom Higgins, who would have loved this book.*

*First published in 1997 by
Obelisk Publications, 2 Church Hill, Pinhoe, Exeter, Devon
Designed by Sally & Chips Barber
Typeset by Sally Barber
Printed in Great Britain by
The Devonshire Press Limited, Torquay, Devon*

HEAVITREE

of Yesteryear

The name 'Heavitree' conjures up different thoughts for different people. For some it will be endless traffic jams but for others it may be their place of birth, home, school, shopping, worship, hospital, soccer, tennis or bowls. For some people it will even bring to mind their favourite beer as the former Heavitree Brewery has spread its name wherever its pubs have been located or its various brewed beers distributed. To people at Alice Springs, in the interior of Australia, the name will be synonymous with a massive rocky outcrop called 'Heavitree Gap'! However, for all those who live or have lived here in Exeter it will mean a mix of all these social factors.

In this small picture postcard book of 'Heavitree of Yesteryear' we shall see how this important part of Exeter looked in the past and greet familiar faces from within, and occasionally from without, the parish. Many of the pictures are taken from Ian Jubb's large collection of Exeter postcards and repeat some of the views included in *Ian Jubb's Exeter Collection*.

Below is the almost-typical view of Heavitree's Fore Street in an age when the amount of through traffic was minimal and crossing the road was not an 'adventure'! In this view there are motor garages on both sides of the road, one next to the Ship and the other, more obvious to see, on the left side just beyond the bakery, where Dunstan's have been for many years. The sign high up on the frontage of the Ship extols the virtues of ales from the Wellpark Brewery. This was located in a red and yellow brick building in Willey's Avenue, a business which started in the 1890s and survived until the 1960s, when many smaller breweries suffered a 'dry death'.

Here we have two views of church towers, one being of the present parish church's impressive tower and the other its pre-

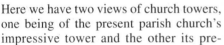

decessor. The 'new' church tower was dedicated in 1890. The design for it attracted more than thirty submissions but the one chosen was from Mr Edward Hall Harbottle from Newcastle-Upon-Tyne. The picture above right shows a crowd gathered for the hoisting of a bell. The church had been rebuilt in stages, the body being the work of David Mackintosh, done in the mid 1840s, a time when Heavitree was growing apace.

The Blessed Sacrament Church is an attractive, even striking, mixture of red brick and stone building, at the top of Fore Street. If you look closely at this pre-Second World War picture you will notice that the church's tower was once much taller than it is now. Damage during the blitz was responsible for its enforced shortening.

The Congregational Church, shown here in two views, is now the United Reformed Church. I wonder how many motorists, and passengers, driving past have noticed the various carefully selected words of wisdom displayed outside, throughout the years? They were started in 1961 by Bob Vanstone of Glenmore Road, a man who started worshipping here in about 1940 and who was a deacon and later an elder. He used to carry scraps of paper around in his pocket and when he saw or thought clever messages he scribbled them down. Some while later they would appear on this building to give passers-by a thought on which to dwell. Just one of hundreds of examples was "Is your life cafeteria-style – self service?" The church is another red brick building dominating the scene in this upper part of Fore Street. The foundation stone for this church, designed by an Exeter architect and built by an Exeter firm, was laid in 1902.

The above view is of the Heavitree Road swimming baths, taken in the 'Pre-Egyptian Age' for now the building has been completely renovated as 'The Pyramids' with an Egyptian theme to add colour to a basic building. The original baths were opened by the Mayor of Exeter, R. Clave Saunders, on 24 May 1939.

Below are two pictures relating to the Martyr Memorial which stands about half way along Denmark Road opposite the Maynard School. The monument is a memorial to two martyrs, Agnes Prest and Thomas Bennet. The bottom left picture shows part of the stake to which the latter was tied when he was burnt to death at Livery Dole.

On the back of the picture postcard above, one of 'Worth's Series' cards, is written "The Liverydale, Heavitree, where Thomas Bennett, MA, was burnt to death for heresy in the year 1531. The lamp adjoining is known as the Gordon Lamp – placed here in memory of his last visit to Exeter, just previous to his going to Egypt." The lamp is a memorial to the famous General Gordon of Khartoum, who died, a hero, in 1885. It stands on the former site of a toll-house, which was demolished the year before the great general was killed. The picture below looks along the last section of Magdalen Road as it heads towards the junction of Fore Street. It shows the almshouses which were built in 1591, and some three years later completed by Sir Robert Dennis. It is believed they were built as penance for the death of Thomas Bennet (the spelling of his surname seeming to vary considerably from historian to historian!) some sixty years earlier. The original sandstone buildings were heavily restored in the mid 19th century, more durable limestone being chosen. However, the chapel of St Clare remains as a sandstone edifice where the ever-busy road forks in two.

8

St Luke's College, in Heavitree Road, is now a part of the University of Exeter. Here are three views to show its front, back and former 'swimming bath and solarium'.

It may well be long gone but people who catch the bus out of Exeter will still ask for 'Heavitree Bridge' and for those of you not yet long enough in the tooth to remember it, here it is, twice! The stream which flowed under it started in a series of springs high in the hills above Whipton and Beacon Heath. Although the stream only had a total length of about four miles, it had a number of names, none of which included Heavitree. In its upper reaches it was referred to as the Mincinglake Brook or the Whipton Brook but locals have, for decades, bestowed their own name of 'The Panny' on it. In the lower reaches it is either known as the Wonford Brook or even the Northbrook so you will have to choose your own preferred option. The stream has undergone an immense transformation since the early part of the 19th century because then it was a crystal clear stream with a healthy fish population and natural banks. Families from Heavitree and Whipton would often visit to picnic beside it, whilst the children tried to catch minnows or tickle trout. However the urban growth of Exeter saw to it that the stream wouldn't keep its rural feel. Instead this small river has been used to carry away storm waters from the built-up areas that have blossomed in its catchment. Whenever there was heavy rain falling on the district the brook would rise alarmingly fast and, in its haste to flow under Heavitree Bridge, would cause deep pools of surface water to form, all too much for wayfarers approaching Exeter along one of the busiest roads into the city. The solution was simple – put the brook into a culvert, out of harm's way. The bridge carried a sign, in the 1930s, warning of a 'Dangerous Corner'.

Heavitree of Yesteryear

The picture above is farther up the same stream at the bottom of Beacon Lane beside Polsloe Bridge. When this was taken, in 1955, the stream was on the surface here but now it's enclosed. The middle and bottom pictures are of the Mote Service Station in the lower part of Fore Street.

The top two pictures are taken between the Mote Service Station and Heavitree Bridge, this being East Wonford Hill or, more precisely, Cross Park Terrace. The top picture is the earlier of the two, the height of the trees and the presence of the tram lines showing the progression. Below is nearby Victor Street.

There aren't too many pubs in Exeter with thatched roofs but this is one of them. Although the Royal Oak has kept much of the same appearance there have been changes. The passageway on the left side has been filled in to become part of the larger building. The cobblestones in front of the inn are no longer visible for there is a tarmacked surface on which cars can park. However there is still an attractive lamp above the door, now stating the name of the pub and still a sign behind that, albeit a different one as it's no longer Priest's Royal Oak Inn.

There was a great welcome procession, with scouts and bands and crowds of people, to herald the opening of the electric tram route from Dunsford Road to Heavitree. Here the gathered assembly are marching down Heavitree's Fore Street.

The next half a dozen pictures of Fore Street are from an age when traffic wasn't as intrusive as it is today. Over the years senior Heavitree citizens have written in to the *Express & Echo* with their memories of what this thoroughfare was like in the past and many were quick to point out that it was possible to play football or rugby in this wide street. How hard that is to imagine these days! The top picture postcard was posted in early 1905 and the middle one, with tram lines, was sent in the following year to Cape Town, South Africa. The message was "Hope you are well. Suppose you will be nice and cool? What price Yorkshire for the championship?" (They came second!)

What a state the roads were in after heavy rain! Both pictures show a serene scene in a place that was yet to be officially a part of 'Greater Exeter'. M. C. B. Hoare recorded his memories of the Heavitree of Yesteryear in the *Express & Echo* in April 1969. He referred to some of the businesses to be found on the left side of this view: "To talk of the Anning family suggests at once bread and confectionery at their little shop just below the corner of North Street where they dispatched a number of toothsome delicacies! There were Mr and Mrs Anning and a sister, Miss Anning, who cheerily accepted every customer alike. They were renowned for their dough cakes but provided a further service which enabled customers to take their own flour, currants, sultanas etc to the shop to be mixed by Mr Anning and then baked in his ovens." The fond recollections also mentioned the nearby premises of Thorne's, the ironmongers, where "Everything under the sun" could be purchased. Both small firms were, at the very least, still trading well into the 1930s according to local directories.

The tram is on the long haul across Exeter to St Thomas and a horse and cart leisurely trundles down the hill. What a peaceful, easy feeling there must have been in Heavitree at one time! The picture shows Langford, the butcher's shop, on one side of the entrance to Regent Street, and the Heavitree Dairy on the other, the latter still retaining a small garden on Fore Street. This postcard view was posted in July 1905 when the electric trams were still something of a novelty. Years ago Heavitree used to stage an annual revel. At such times there was much merrymaking. Edward J. Scoble had these reminiscences published in the *Express & Echo* in July 1962: "There was an influx of

16

a certain class of people from the neighbouring city of Exeter… Special trestle tables were put up in the yard of the Ship Inn and there was plenty of beer consumed in the pubs… This was followed on the Tuesday and Wednesday by the fair when stalls were put up in the streets … the highlight was the races which took place in the main street, and also the climbing of the greasy pole. This was erected on the pavement by the Ship Inn. I believe the last time it was climbed was by a baker who worked for Mr Gifford. He failed in his first attempt, so got a bag of ashes from the bakehouse and rubbed it in the grease. What a mess! But he got his leg of mutton!"

Church Street is the scene for these two pictures from Edwardian times. Everybody is wearing their 'Sunday Best' as various carriages are waiting to set off. The view below is a less populated one with several people standing to gaze at the photographer at work. Above the shop on the left is the name 'F. Hodges' with the additional information 'J. Gifford, cook and confectioner' below that. Today it is that fine shop 'Westward Rentals'! (Ok Eddie?) The sender mentioned in his 1909 note, on the back of this view card, that 'Harry' was standing "Half way down the street". The top picture on the opposite page shows the street from a different angle. The tram, again the subject of the next two cards, has progressed up Fore Street in these pictures from the 'Pre-Traffic Light Age'. The middle card was published to commemorate their arrival on 4 April 1905. The picture below that shows how much more narrow the top end of Fore Street was, the properties on the right having substantial gardens in front of them.

18

The picture at the top shows a motor accident, in 1938, at Livery Dole, where the traffic lights are on the junction of Polsloe and Heavitree Roads. Where the buildings are located, behind the crashed car, is now a flower bed. Beside and below are views looking up the top end of Fore Street. The card to the right didn't travel too far, being posted, on 20 October 1903, to the Rev Barton Lee at 35 Cross Park Terrace in Heavitree.

These two views are away from the shopping centre, the top one being of South Lawn Terrace when the road was much narrower than it is today.
Below, a group of men posed for the photographer, at the cemetery end of Chard Road when it was being developed. The scene hasn't changed greatly but there are now houses at the junction with Hamlin Lane.

Heavitree Park has, over the years, seen plenty of children and adults enjoy many different activities. Before the tennis courts were introduced there was a football pitch on the same spot; newspapers reported that the soccer matches between Heavitree United and Heavitree Unionists were 'hard-fought epics'. The top picture is the older of these two, there being no houses in Whipton Lane, giving an unimpaired view of the rears of Cross Park Terrace! The date of the middle picture is August 1935. Below is the playing field at Bramdean School. The bottom picture, opposite, is Newcombe Street at the beginning of the 20th century.

Heavitree United have a long and proud history in local soccer. In the next few pages are several teams from down the years. On this page two of the teams from the 1920s are featured, the lower one having some of the personnel from above. This one had the players listed so, for the record, the back row (L to R) was: H. Liddicoat, J. Geary, P. Cavey, F. Blackmore, W. Isaac, S. Wilcox, E. Hodge and F. Moore. Middle Row: R. A. G. Daltry (Hon Sec), H. Anning, W. Shute (Vice Capt), W. Lowton, Rev A. Seymour (Vice-Chairman), L. Ralph (Chairman), R. Brown (Hon Treas), E. Ousley, H. Geary and R. James (Assist Hon Sec). Front Row: W. Borne, B. Stevens, E. Symes, H. Arscott (Capt), A. J. Westaway (Acting Hon Vice-Pres), G. Liddicoat, W. Mortimore, F. Harrold F. Lendon.

The three teams shown opposite are, from top to bottom, from the 1933/34, 1946/47 and 1951/52 seasons. The young man immediately to the left of the larger trophy is Alan Greenwell, who was my Geography teacher at the Episcopal School in Exeter. He must have done a good job as I went on to spend many years teaching Geography myself, at the Vincent Thompson High School (now St Luke's) on the edge of Heavitree.

Heavitree of Yesteryear

These houses on the lower slopes of East Wonford Hill, on the left of this picture, were the subject of much controversy in the first half of the 1960s when it was deemed that they should be demolished as part of a road widening scheme. Some eminent people, including W. G. Hoskins, fought their cause as at least one of them, a Queen Anne house, was worthy of preservation. In February 1961 Mr and Mrs Mead and their four children moved out to take up residence in another part of Heavitree. Over the following years, and whilst the properties became decayed and vandalised, the arguments raged. In 1966 they were still debating the matter. However now they have gone and the traffic still tails back down East Wonford Hill each day. One of the more unusual features lost here was that of a 'Highwayman's Step', this being a purposely contrived irregular step which would cause would-be intruders to stumble. Below is a picture of the Gardeners Arms in Wonford, taken many years before it was rebuilt in the 1930s.

Probably nothing has done more to perpetuate the name 'Heavitree' than the famous brewery which stood in Church Street. Although the buildings have been demolished for a sheltered housing development, aptly called 'The Maltings', the company continues to thrive and still oversees more than a hundred pubs across the region. Their headquarters are at Trood House, not far from Matford on the outskirts of Exeter, and were established there in 1984 when the old brewery site was

cleared for redevelopment. The company's history has been one of constant change. John Wolland started a malting business in Church Street in 1750 and by 1790 had expanded into brewing. This was continued by his nephew William whose own son, Thomas, carried on from there. His sister, Elizabeth, married Thomas Baker, who joined the firm in 1837, then known as the 'Heavitree Family Brewery'. Poor Thomas's association was short-lived for he died that same year. However Elizabeth, along with her son, Robert, stayed with the firm, 'Baker & Son', until 1890. It was then that it became the Heavitree Brewery Limited. This was an era of expansion, the vibrant firm buying from the Crowson family, in 1899, the nearby Windsor Brewery, which was sited in Heavitree's North Street. Having bought one of its competitors, it shut the Windsor Brewery down in 1902. The expansion continued apace with the acquisition of both Finch's Eagle Brewery in Exeter and Pinsent's of Newton Abbot. However, in business, as in life itself, nothing runs smoothly all the time and there were setbacks. One occurred in January 1916 with the appointment of Mr Gall as Secretary and General Manager. Despite being awarded an excellent salary, he systematically robbed the company and by 1922 had reduced it to financial ruin. He fled to Canada but was caught and returned to face the music. He was found guilty and served three years' penal servitude. The firm's saviour came in the shape of John Parnell Tucker, a major creditor, who acquired a controlling shareholding. He boosted the firm's prospects by enlisting the help of his brewing friend, H. C. Hammans, who had just sold his own brewing business in Andover. Together these men quickly came to the rescue of the Heavitree Brewery and, within a short time, the business of buying up other local breweries again began in earnest. However, in 1970 the brewing of beer ceased at the Church Street brewery, thereby ending a tradition that had continued through several generations. The bottom two pictures were taken after the brewery buildings had been demolished but before work started on The Maltings.

This pair of pictures takes us even farther from the heart of Heavitree, the views being of Ladysmith Road and Ladysmith School. The top view shows a rare scene, which it would be today, of a road with not a single vehicle in it. In the bottom picture a group have gathered around the flag pole where Captain Vaughan is addressing the children and visitors at the "Heavitree Council Schools' ceremony of unfurling the Union Jack". As all good citizens will know, the caption should have said 'The Union Flag'! The message on the back of this postcard said, "With a magnifying glass I am 3 from the steps, then Arthur, you (minus a head) and then Nellie but it is rather indistinct. I visited the school today and inspected the needlework, heard history and played with the babies."

St Luke's High School sits on the edge of Heavitree and many children from the parish have been educated there. This picture shows fourteen members of staff, when the school was known as Vincent Thompson High School. Some (at the time of writing) are still there, some have sadly passed on, whilst others have moved on to different careers, including myself and John Lloyd.

Below is the school football team which played at St James' Park in the 1978 final of the East Devon schools cup tournament. The result was a 0-0 draw with Hele's School (now St Peter's), the teams sharing the trophy, presented by Exeter City's Peter Hatch.

The buildings are the same but the businesses are not! Here we have a familiar run of shops in the upper part of Fore Street. In the bottom picture there is no post office because that was located, at least in the 1930s, at what used to be number 11 Fore Street (now number 56) immediately below the Ship Inn (now the Ship & Pelican). The building in this picture with 'Exeter Bank' on the window is now Rogers News, quite possibly where you bought this book!

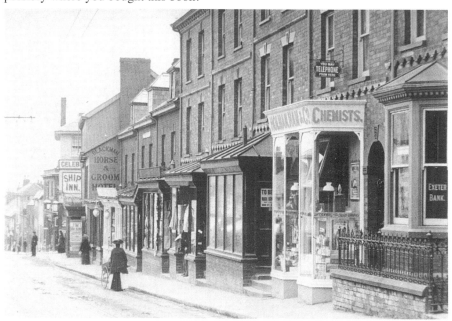